THE CUP
OF BLESSING

Sharing Communion as a Family

THE CUP
OF BLESSING

Sharing Communion as a Family

by

Larry Huggins

HARRISON HOUSE
Tulsa, Oklahoma

06 05 04 03 02   10 9 8 7 6 5 4 3 2 1

The Cup of Blessing—
Sharing Communion as a Family
ISBN 1-57794-546-8
Copyright © 2002 by Larry Huggins
3930 Glade Road, #108-387
Colleyville, TX 76034 USA

Published by Harrison House, Inc.
P.O. Box 35035
Tulsa, Oklahoma 74153

Contents

Acknowledgments

Had it not been for the encouragement of my publisher and life-long friend, Keith Provance, I may never have become a published author. He literally squeezed my first two books out of me.

Over the years, however, I have mellowed out. He merely pointed out the need for this book and suggested that I write it—there was no pressure. It was a blessing to write. Thank You, Keith.

I would also like to thank Keith and his wife, Megan, for helping raise my sons. You deposited many of their better qualities.

Dedication

To my wife and partner, Loretta

1

Family Communion— A Living Experience

When my beautiful wife, Loretta, and I were newlyweds, we prayerfully wrote down all the things that we wanted in our marriage. At the top of the list we wrote, "We will have family communion as often as we are lead."

We wrote "as often as we are lead," because we wanted our family communion to be a *living experience* rather than *a dead tradition*. We did not say every Sunday or the first day of each month because we did not want to set unrealistic goals.

We have gone through periods when we celebrated family communion every day.

We once celebrated family communion thirty-six times in six weeks. We called it our "Month of Sundays." Each communion service was unique and more glorious than the previous service, and those services changed our lives.

Several times we have had family communion more than once a day because we needed it. Sometimes we have gone weeks without having communion.

However, I believe more is better than less. Remember this: *Seven days without the Lord's Table makes one weak.*

On many occasions we have family communion by long distance. Loretta has her elements at home while I have mine in some far away place. We share the Word of God over the telephone and rejoice just like we are in the same room.

A few years ago the *LeSea Broadcasting Network* asked me to hold family communion services on live television. We had ten hours of live, family communion over a five-day period. I invited the television audience to take juice and bread and join us in celebrating the Lord's Table.

Each night the telephone lines would light up with praise reports from thankful people. Many said they had never taken communion at home. Some said their churches seldom, if ever, took communion. People joyously reported salvation, healing, restoration, and reconciliation of their families and marriages.

I began to see more clearly the blessings people missed in the absence of family communion.

Begin to celebrate family communion right away. As you do, new doorways of blessings will open unto you and your loved ones.

Family communion does not exempt you from receiving communion among your church community. Be faithful and bloom where you are planted.

This handbook is not meant to be a ritual. Don't follow it blindly. It simply offers a few insights and suggestions that will help you step onto a path of revelation that will bless you and your loved ones immeasurably.

As always, allow the Holy Spirit to guide you in your own celebration of family communion.

WHO CAN SERVE COMMUNION?

You may be wondering if it is acceptable for a layman to celebrate communion in his own household. Shouldn't a priest or cleric administer the sacerdotal rites?

Many religious orders and denominations allow only ordained ministers or priests to serve at the Lord's Table. Such organizations are within their rights to place restrictions on official, church-sanctioned services. We respect their choices; however, outside of their individual traditions or creeds, there is no biblical basis for such limitations.

Any believer can celebrate family communion in his own home, anytime he chooses. In fact, the Word of God encourages family communion.

And they, continuing daily with one accord in the temple, and breaking bread from house to house, did eat their meat with gladness and singleness of heart.

Acts 2:46

Notice two things about this verse:

(1) They worshipped God publicly, in the temple.

(2) They broke bread from house to house, every day.

This practice was known as the Apostle's Doctrine. The apostles received their instructions regarding communion directly from Jesus Himself.

> And as they did eat, *Jesus* took bread, and blessed, and brake it, and gave to them, and *said*, Take, eat: this is my body.
>
> And he took the cup, and when he had given thanks, he gave it to them: and they all drank of it.
>
> And he said unto them, This is my blood of the new testament, which is shed for many.
>
> Mark 14:22-24

Notice the phrase, "which is shed for many." The Lord's Table has never been limited to just a few, special people. The Gospel would not be Good News if it were not available to everyone. God has extended an open invitation, "...*whosoever* will, let him take the water of life freely" (Rev. 22:17). *Whosoever* means *you!*

Certainly Jesus was speaking of the Holy Sacraments when He said, "*Whoso* eateth my flesh, and drinketh my blood, hath eternal life; and I will raise him up at the last day" (John 6:54). *Whoso* is another way of saying anyone.

Jesus also defended David for sharing hallowed, priestly bread with his soldiers. "And he [Jesus] said unto them, Have ye never read what David did, when he had need, and was an hungred, he, and they that were with him? How he went into the house of God in the days of Abiathar the high priest, and did eat the shewbread, which is not lawful to eat but for the priests, and gave also to them which were with him?" (Mark 2:25-26).

David was not the king at this time, and this happened under the Old Testament. Yet Jesus taught that it was acceptable for these men to eat the sacred bread.

Historically, the Lord's Table of the New Testament originated in the Old Testament as the Passover Supper, or the Feast of Unleavened Bread, which was an ordinance to be observed forever. (Ex. 12:14.) Exodus 12:3 says, "Speak ye unto all the congregation of Israel, saying, In the tenth day of this month they shall take to them every man a lamb, according to the house of their fathers, *a lamb for an house.*"

If you read this entire account you will notice it says every person was commanded to participate in the Passover feast; either in his own household or his neighbor's household. Individual priests were not assigned to oversee the Passover supper in *every* house. This event took place before the Jewish priesthood was instituted. There were no priests available.

While it is true that God sets priests as ministry gifts in the church, what do you do when they are unavailable? You do not need a priest in your home to read God's Word for you. You do not need an ordained minister in your home to pray your prayers for you. Likewise, you can celebrate family communion, on your own, in your own home.

Today, in New Testament times, every believer has been promoted into the priesthood. "And [Jesus] hath made us kings and *priests* unto God and his Father" (Rev. 1:6). God recognizes the family priest. After all, He instituted the family *before* He instituted the church. Therefore every believer can preside over his own personal family communion in his own household.

Of course, this does not license you to preside in the public assembly if your local assembly requires communion be led by an ordained and/or licensed minister. Ministering communion in your own home is different than ministering communion in public services. Your sphere of authority does not necessarily extend into the public assembly. Some church organizations allow only their duly appointed ministers serve communion on church property. Please respect your church organization's creed.

However, you should be the priest over your own household. It is your duty to lead your family in the things of God—Scripture reading, devotionals, prayer, and family communion.

WHAT ABOUT THE ELEMENTS?

In many churches wine is served, while in other churches grape juice is used. This is a matter of custom and personal conviction. You must decide which is appropriate for your household.

In lieu of regular communion supplies Loretta and I have used apple juice, orange juice, and even water. Jesus turned water into wine. I believe the prayer of thanksgiving makes the contents of the cup acceptable. Communion is a matter of the heart.

Some churches use special wafers made just for communion and others use crackers or unleavened bread. Again, it is a matter of personal preference and sometimes necessity. Loretta and I have used every kind of bread imaginable, including macaroni and corn chips. My philosophy is make do with what you have!

Likewise, you do not need a silver chalice or crystal glasses, but if you have them and want to use them, be free. Perhaps you have seen people drink from a common, communion cup. I have done that, but I prefer my own cup. If all you have are paper cups, I am sure the Lord will not mind.

You can also go to a Christian bookstore and buy your communion supplies. You can even buy a personal, traveling communion kit, which is very convenient.

Smith Wigglesworth, a legendary man of faith, traveled with a small, personal communion kit. It was his practice to have communion daily, no matter where he was.

Jesus taught about celebrating communion often: "For as *often* as ye eat this bread, and drink this cup, ye do shew the Lord's death till he come" (1 Cor. 11:26). Notice the word *often*.

Luke reported that the early church had communion every day. "And they, continuing *daily* with one accord in the temple, and breaking bread from house to house, did eat their meat with gladness and singleness of heart..." (Acts 2:46).

It is unlikely that you will ever run the risk of having family communion too often. You will be

sure to keep it meaningful if you guard your heart
and remain sincere.

2

The Basics of Communion

Jesus taught that the bread represents His body and the wine represents His blood.

> ...the Lord Jesus the same night in which he was betrayed *took bread:*

> And when he had given thanks, he brake it, and said, Take, eat: this is my body, which is broken for you: this do in remembrance of me.

> After the same manner also he *took the cup,* when he had supped, saying, This cup is the new testament in my blood: this do ye, as oft as ye drink it, in remembrance of me.

> 1 Corinthians 11:23-25

It is important to remember two fundamental truths that Jesus taught about communion:

(1) His body was battered and bruised so our bodies can be whole.

(2) His blood was shed to ratify the New Covenant.

Jesus said the bread and the wine should be taken in remembrance of Him. (1 Cor. 11:24-25.) This means to repeatedly call to mind. Communion reminds us of what Jesus did for us in His sacrifice:

(1) He suffered spirit, soul, and body.

(2) He conquered death, hell, and the grave.

(3) He entered into the Holy of Holies with His own blood to atone for us, eternally.

There is more to the Lord's Table than eating bread and drinking wine. There is a revelation of

Jesus Christ. Each time we celebrate communion we will see a different facet of Jesus. The apostle Paul's revelation of the Lord's Table is found in 1 Corinthians 11:23: "For *I have received of the Lord* that which also I delivered unto you, that the Lord Jesus the same night in which he was betrayed took bread...."

Paul did not receive this teaching from seminary or catechism. The other apostles did not teach him about communion. Jesus Himself revealed the mysteries of communion to Paul. Notice, Paul said, "I have received of the Lord...." This tells us that communion is not a man-made tradition. The Lord Jesus instituted the sacrament and He perpetuates it.

Communion is not merely about symbolism or types and shadows. Communion is not just about forgiveness. There is more to it than we have realized.

Every time we celebrate communion we give Jesus an opportunity to reveal Himself. When conducted in the proper, *spiritual* attitude, communion eliminates everything that clouds our awareness of Christ. When unforgiveness and pride go out, Jesus comes in.

On the same day that Jesus was resurrected He appeared to two men who were walking to the village of Emmaus. Jesus walked with them and shared the Scriptures with them for hours, but they did not recognize Him. Later that evening they invited Him to join them for supper.

> And it came to pass, as he sat at meat with them, he took bread, and blessed it, and brake, and gave to them.
>
> *And their eyes were opened, and they knew him;* and he vanished out of their sight.

> Luke 24:30-31

They did not recognize Him until *after* He broke the bread and blessed it. (This is a good reason to pray over your food.)

What Does Communion Mean?

The Greek word for communion, *koinonia*, has several shades of meaning: partnership, sharing, or communication. In the New Testament it is often rendered *fellowship*. "The cup of blessing which we bless, is it not the *communion* of the blood of Christ? The bread which we break, is it not the communion of the body of Christ?" (1 Cor. 10:16).

Communion is fellowship. Fellowship is sharing in His benefits or being partakers of Christ—heavenly communication. "God is faithful, by whom ye were called unto the fellowship [koinonia] of his Son Jesus Christ our Lord" (1 Cor. 1:9).

You will discover many things as you further explore the mysteries of communion. The more you partake of the Lord's Table, the more He will reveal Himself to you. Your inheritance is waiting to be uncovered.

Your spiritual hunger will lead you to the Lord's Table. "Blessed are they, which do hunger and thirst after righteousness: for they shall be filled" (Matt. 5:6).

Your spiritual hunger will be fulfilled at the Lord's Table. "For he satisfieth the longing soul, and filleth the hungry soul with goodness" (Ps. 107:9).

You will uncover your inheritance at the Lord's Table. "Thou preparest a table before me in the presence of mine enemies: thou anointest my head with oil; my cup runneth over. Surely goodness and mercy shall follow me all the days of my life: and I will dwell in the house of the Lord for ever" (Ps. 23:5-6).

Look at the benefits that come as you partake of the Lord's Table:

(1) Protection from your adversaries

(2) The anointing of the priest and the king

(3) Supernatural abundance

(4) Abundant life

(5) Tender mercy

(6) Security

(7) Royal sonship

We get the words *community* and *communion* from the same word, *common*.[1] The family of God is also referred to as the body of Christ. We are a family, or community, of believers and we are united through Christ. "Now ye are the body of Christ, and members in particular" (1 Cor. 12:27).

We, the body of Christ, individually and collectively, are in partnership with one another and

God through communion. "That which we have seen and heard declare we unto you, that ye also may have fellowship *with us:* and truly our fellowship is *with the Father,* and *with his Son* Jesus Christ" (1 John 1:3).

For many people God is somewhere far away. Communion promotes God-on-the-inside consciousness. It celebrates the fact that God is inside of us and we are in God. This is the most intimate of fellowship.

He that eateth my flesh, and drinketh my blood, dwelleth in me, and I in him.

As the living Father hath sent me, and I live by the Father: so he that eateth me, even he shall live by me.

This is that bread which came down from heaven: not as your fathers did eat manna, and are dead: he that eateth of this bread shall live for ever.

John 6:56-58

This is why we must guard ourselves against sin and wrong attitudes. If our partnership is hindered at any level, it restricts the flow of God's blessings.

GROW UP SPIRITUALLY

There are three reasons why it is important that we not break fellowship:

(1) If we break fellowship with our brethren, it hinders our relationship with God.

(2) If we break fellowship with God, it hinders our fellowship with our brethren.

If we break fellowship in any area it impedes our spiritual development.

Wherefore whosoever shall eat this bread, and drink this cup of the Lord, unworthily,[2] shall be guilty of the body and blood of the Lord.

But let a man examine himself, and so let him eat of that bread, and drink of that cup.

For he that eateth and drinketh unworthily, eateth and drinketh damnation[3] to himself, not discerning[4] the Lord's body.

For this cause many are weak and sickly among you, and many sleep.

For if we would judge[5] ourselves, we should not be judged.[6]

But when we are judged, we are chastened[7] of the Lord, that we should not be condemned[8] with the world.

1 Corinthians 11:27-32

Remember these important points about family communion:

(1) Family communion is a time of self-exami-nation and self-correction. It is not a time for correcting others.

(2) Family communion is a time to receive divine instruction and revelation.

(3) Family communion is a time of being aware of everything that Christ accomplished for us.

(4) Family communion is a time of forgiveness and reconciliation.

(5) Family communion is a time for restoration and unity.

(6) Family communion is a joyous time of fellowship with God.

(7) Any time is a good time for communion.

(8) Anything that hinders our partnership with God or other believers is simply a call to family communion.

For many believers, communion has always been a very solemn event. While we always conduct ourselves reverently, family communion does not have to be dull. It is a celebration of life. "He brought me to the banqueting house, and his banner over me was love" (Song of Solomon 2:4).

Family communion can range from a morsel to a banquet. The Passover Feast was a love banquet, not just a snack. This practice was carried into the Lord's Table of the New Testament. Many times in the Epistles communion is called a feast.

At the Last Supper, after He had blessed the bread and the wine, Jesus said, "drink ye all of it" (Matt 26:27). I don't believe He would have said that about a tiny wafer and a thimble of wine.

The Lord's Table should be for reverencing God, not merely enjoying a meal. Paul had to correct the Corinthian believers for being irreverent. Some were intemperately gorging themselves before the other members were even seated at the banqueting table. Paul said, "This is not how to have communion. One remains hungry while the other gets drunk!" (1 Cor. 11:20-21 author's paraphrase.)

Family communion should be enjoyable. It is not a time to center on the flesh but to center on Jesus. According to the Gospel of John, many things took place at the Last Supper. It took four chapters to describe everything that happened in that first communion service. (John 13-17 describes everything that happened in and around that Passover feast.)

Besides the eating and drinking there was a foot-washing service; lots of praying, preaching, and prophesying; a warning of betrayal, (and the exposing of a betrayer); more warnings; a forecast of the Holy Spirit's ministry; several new commandments; a divine impartation of peace; insight into demonic activity; the entire sermon of the True Vine; special instructions; several divine revelations and intercessory prayers, all in one event.

John omitted the song service, but Matthew did not. "And when they had *sung an hymn*, they went out into the Mount of Olives" (Matt. 26:30).

A lot can happen during family communion. Always be sensitive to the Holy Spirit and to others. "Wherefore, my brethren, when ye come together to eat, *tarry one for another*" (1 Cor. 11:33).

> *Rejoice* with them that do rejoice, and *weep* with them that weep.
>
> **Romans 12:15**

There are only two states in any family communion service. The following Scripture is almost identical to the previous verse. "Is any among you afflicted? let him *pray*. Is any merry? let him *sing psalms*" (James 5:13). Rejoicing corresponds to singing, and weeping corresponds to prayer.

As in any service, you need to know what to do and when to do it. Remember these simple rules of thumb and you will always be on target in your family communion.

We do not begin family communion until everyone present is ready to start.

(1) We are not through until everyone is through.

(2) We deal with sorrow or affliction through prayer.

(3) We are not done until we are all free enough to truly praise God in song.

PRACTICAL ADVICE FOR FAMILY COMMUNION

You can have personal communion with the Lord any time you choose. There are no scriptural prohibitions against it. However, this book is about family communion. Here is some advice that will help you.

Communion is for born-again believers. The Scriptures teach that light cannot fellowship with darkness. (Eph. 5:11.) This does not mean that we cannot live with and love the unbelievers in our household. However, by definition they cannot be partakers of Christ's body unless they are in the body of Christ.

There is an old saying: we do not count our money in front of the poor or eat our bread in front of the hungry. If there are unbelievers in your household, be sensitive to them. Your actions can draw them in or drive them away. You have three choices:

(1) Lead them to the Lord.

(2) Have communion when they are not present.

(3) Give them opportunity to either remove themselves voluntarily or observe *reverently* while you worship God.

If you are not the head of the household, you must have the consent of the head of the household, or limit your family communion to a private area where you have liberty to conduct your celebration of communion.

Where you have liberty, enjoy it. However, whenever possible, adjust your conduct to your circumstances. For example, do not disturb your neighbors by being too loud. Any altercation that might ensue will shift the focus away from Jesus, and that defeats the purpose.

Where children are involved, and I hope they are, explain the facts to them.

(1) Family communion is for believers.

(2) Family communion is about Jesus.

(3) Family communion is worship.

Some churches have age restrictions for young people to receive communion. Family communion is different. It takes place in your household. If your four-year-old loves Jesus and is well behaved, he may participate in family communion.

Young children have a very short attention span, so adjust the length of your family communion accordingly. Likewise, simplify the concepts you discuss with your children. You will be amazed at how well they grasp deep, spiritual concepts.

Sometimes you can plan for family communion and other times it will be spontaneous. Be ready for either circumstance. Go with the flow. Turn off the TV and disconnect the telephone so that the focus is on Jesus.

Gather your little congregation around you and settle them down. You can begin with a prayer, a song, or a Scripture. Get out the Bible, the elements, and celebrate family communion.

The following chapter offers some seed-thoughts for family communion. I encourage you to write down your own family communion ideas. The Holy Spirit will also give you many ideas. His supply is inexhaustible and always appropriate for every situation.

Enjoy your family communion.

3

~

Suggested Family Communion Services

I recommend that you always use a familiar, communion text, such as these below, and keep your Bible marked to 1 Corinthians 11:23-24, John 6:56-58, and Mark 14:22-24.

Connect the communion text with a supporting text from the outline or your own selection to establish the theme for your family communion.

You will find comments and questions in the family communion outlines to help you get started. Do not feel as though you have to stay with the outline. Follow the Holy Spirit's leading.

The summaries are to help you end your family communion. Again, trust the Holy Spirit to lead you.

Abiding in Christ

Jesus on the Inside, Showing on the Outside

Supporting Text: John 15:4-8 [Study all four verses]

Abide in me, **and I in you. As the branch cannot bear fruit of itself, except it abide in the vine; no more can ye, except ye abide in me....**

Comments & Questions:

- Jesus is the vine.

- We are the branches.

- Where does life come from?

- Where does the fruit grow?

- What happens if the branch is broken off?

- What might hinder the life from flowing?

- How can we keep the life flowing to the branch?

Summary: Because we are in the body of Jesus, His life can flow through us, producing fruit in every area: spiritually, in the soul (mind, will, and emotions), and physically. As we partake of the bread and the wine we are receiving life from the True Vine.

ABUNDANCE

It Is His Good Pleasure to Give Us the Kingdom

Supporting Text: 1 Peter 1:18-19

Forasmuch as ye know that ye were not redeemed with corruptible things, as silver and gold, from your vain conversation received by tradition from your fathers; But with *the precious blood of Christ,* as of a lamb without blemish and without spot.

Supporting Text: Romans 8:32

He that spared not his own Son, but delivered him up for us all, how shall he not with him *also freely give us all things?*

Comments & Questions:

- The blood of Jesus is priceless.

- Jesus purchased us with His blood.

- What makes the blood of Jesus special?

- What makes you special?

- Do you believe God will provide for you?

Summary: Because Jesus' blood was shed for us, we know we are valuable to God. As we partake of the bread, the body, and the wine, the blood, we are certain He will always provide for us. The Lord's Table is a table of abundance.

BOLDNESS

We Are Sons of God and Citizens of Heaven

Supporting Text: Hebrews 4:14-16

Seeing then that we have a great high priest, that is passed into the heavens, Jesus the Son of God, let us hold fast our profession. For we have not an high priest which cannot be touched with the feeling of our infirmities; but was in all points tempted like as we are, yet without sin. Let us therefore *come boldly* unto the throne of grace, that we may obtain mercy, and find grace to help in time of need.

Comments & Questions:

* Jesus has all the qualities we need.

* All His qualities are resident in His blood.

- What kinds of temptations, tests, and trials did Jesus undergo?

- Does Jesus understand what you are going through?

- When God sees the blood of Jesus in our lives, what does He see?

Summary: As we receive the body and the blood of Jesus, we become partakers of His divine nature: goodness, purity, power, victory, wisdom, and righteousness (and the righteous are bold as lions).

BETRAYAL

He Sticks Closer Than a Brother

Supporting Text: Matthew 26:1-2

And it came to pass, when Jesus had finished all these sayings, he said unto his disciples,

Ye know that after two days is the feast of the passover, and *the Son of man is betrayed* to be crucified.

Comments & Questions:

* A friend, Judas, betrayed Jesus.

* All, even His closest followers, abandoned Him.

* Jesus never abandoned His friends.

* What must it have been like for Jesus to be completely alone?

* Have you ever felt betrayed?

* Who is most important in your life, Jesus or others?

* Will Jesus ever abandon you?

Summary: Because Jesus was abandoned (even forsaken briefly by His Father), we will never have to be alone. As we partake of His body and blood, we are reminded that we are in Him and He is in us. He will abide with us forever.

BLOOD SPEAKS

All Things Are Purged by Blood

Supporting Text: Hebrews 12:22-24 [Study all three verses]

...And to Jesus the mediator of the new covenant, and to the blood of sprinkling, that *speaketh better things* than that of Abel.

Supporting Text: Hebrews 9:24

For Christ is not entered into the holy places made with hands, which are the figures of the true; *but into heaven itself,* now to appear in the presence of God for us.

Comments & Questions:

* Nothing speaks more to God than the blood of Jesus.

- Jesus entered heaven with His own blood to make atonement for us.

- What is more important to God: the enemy's accusations or intercessions of Jesus?

- What are some things the blood of Jesus is saying on our behalf right now?

Summary: This bread and this cup of the New Testament speaks to God. As we celebrate family communion, the blood of Jesus is speaking on our behalf saying, *these have been declared righteous.* If God says we are right, then we are!

CLEANSING

He Will Wash Sin Right Out of Your Life!

Supporting Text: 1 John 1:6-10

If we say that we have fellowship with him, and walk in darkness, we lie, and do not the

truth: **But if we walk in the light, as he is in the light, we have fellowship one with another, and *the blood of Jesus Christ his Son cleanseth us* from all sin....**

Comments & Questions:

- Walking in the light is walking in the Word.

- As we walk in the light, the blood of Jesus cleanses us from all sin.

- Do you know anyone who has never sinned?

- Can anyone be cleansed by avoiding God's light?

- Is it better to run from God's light, or to run to God's light?

- Is there any sin that the blood of Jesus cannot cleanse?

Summary: As we come to the Lord's Table, in obedience to the Word of God, we come into His light. As we are in the light, the blood of Jesus cleanses us of all sin. Thank God for the body and the cleansing blood of Jesus.

DELIVERANCE

Yea, Though I Walk Through the Valley....

Supporting Text: John 3:20-21

For *every one that doeth evil hateth the light,* neither cometh to the light, lest his deeds should be reproved. But he that doeth truth cometh to the light, that his deeds may be made manifest, that they are wrought in God.

Supporting Text: Colossians 1:12-13

Giving thanks unto the Father, which hath made us meet to be partakers of the inheritance of the saints in light: Who hath *delivered us from the power of darkness,* and hath translated us into the kingdom of his dear Son.

Comments & Questions:

- Evil spirits and evil men run from God's light.

- We are now the saints in light.

- Are you safest hiding in the shadows or walking in the light?

- How can you get into God's light?

Summary: As we partake of His flesh and blood we are reminded that Jesus is the light of the world. Because we are in Jesus and He is in us, we have become the children of light. Darkness flees from the light!

FORGIVENESS

Let Go and Let God Take Care of It

Supporting Text: 1 Corinthians 11:28-29

But *let a man examine himself,* and so let him eat of that bread, and drink of that cup. For he that eateth and drinketh unworthily, eateth and drinketh damnation to himself, not discerning the Lord's body.

Supporting Text: Matthew 6:14-15

For if ye forgive men their trespasses, *your heavenly Father will also forgive you:* But if ye forgive not men their trespasses, neither will your Father forgive your trespasses.

Comments & Questions:

- Unforgiveness is faith's greatest hindrance.

- Our forgiveness is based upon forgiving others.

- How many times has God forgiven you?

- Can you afford not to forgive others?

Summary: As we partake of these elements we are reminded that Jesus forgave those who sent Him to the cross. We hereby release all who have offended or hurt us, receive forgiveness for ourselves, and enter unhindered fellowship with Jesus and the body of Christ.

FUTURE

He Has the Whole World in His Hands

Supporting Text: Hebrews 12:2

Looking unto Jesus *the author and finisher of our faith*; who for the joy that was set before him endured the cross, despising the shame, and is set down at the right hand of the throne of God.

Supporting Text: John 16:13-15 [Study all three verses]

Howbeit when he, the Spirit of truth, is come, he will guide you into all truth: for he shall not speak of himself; but whatsoever he shall hear, that shall he speak: and *he will shew you things to come....*

Comments & Questions:

- Jesus could see beyond the dark day of Calvary.

- Jesus knows your future, and it is bright.

- What did Jesus see beyond the cross?

- What things do you know He has in store for you?

Summary: When Jesus broke bread, He said, "I will not drink henceforth of this fruit of the vine, until that day when I drink it new with you in my Father's kingdom" (Matt. 26:29). That day is now. He saw this day (and all our tomorrows). We are partaking of our future and celebrating all the promises that are sure to come.

HEALING

The Great Physician Makes House Calls

Supporting Text: 1 Corinthians 11:28-30 [Study all three verses]

...For this cause many are weak and sickly among you, and many sleep.

Supporting Text: Matthew 14:36

And besought him that they might only touch the hem of his garment: and *as many as touched were made perfectly whole.*

Comments & Questions:

- Healing can take place during communion.

- It is always God's will for us to come to Him for healing.

- What could prevent you from being healed?

- Is there any unforgiveness in your heart?

- What virtues are in the sacraments?

Summary: People who merely touched Jesus garment were healed. How much more virtue is in His body and blood? As we partake of the bread and the wine, we are reminded *His wounds healed us.* Therefore we celebrate the fact that His healing virtue is in us now, restoring us and preserving our health.

HOLY SPIRIT

He Will Pour in the Oil and the Wine

Supporting Text: John 14:16-19 [Study all four verses]

...I will not leave you comfortless: I will come to you. Yet a little while, and the world seeth

me no more; but ye see me: because I live, ye shall live also.

[See also John 16:7]

Supporting Text: Romans 14:17

For the kingdom of God is not meat and drink; but righteousness, and peace, and *joy in the Holy Ghost*.

Comments & Questions:

- During the Last Supper, Jesus promised to send His Holy Spirit to be with us.

- The Holy Spirit has replaced Jesus' earthly presence.

- What does the Holy Spirit do in our lives today?

- As we fellowship in the Holy Spirit, with whom are we fellowshipping?

Summary: Today we are reminded that our Lord's Table is more than eat and drink. It is joy in the Holy Spirit. As we partake of the bread and the wine we recognize the communion of the Holy Spirit. He abides with us forever.

LOVE

They'll Know We Are Christians by Our Love

Supporting Text: John 13:34-35

A new commandment I give unto you, That ye love one another; **as I have loved you, that ye also love one another. By this shall all men know that ye are my disciples, if ye have love one to another.**

Supporting Text: John 15:12-14 [Study all three verses]

...Greater love hath no man than this, **that a man lay down his life for his friends. Ye are my friends, if ye do whatsoever I command you.**

Comments & Questions:

- The Ten Commandments have been superseded by one commandment.

- God is love and we are recreated in His likeness.

- Have you been walking the love walk towards all brethren?

- In what areas are you tempted to step out of love?

Summary: This table is proof that the Lord loves us unconditionally. He laid His life down for us when we were not lovable. As we partake of this love feast we recognize His love for us and we reaffirm our love for His body.

MEMORIES

Get a Check-up

Supporting Text: Hebrews 9:14

How much more shall the blood of Christ, who through the eternal Spirit offered himself without spot to God, purge your conscience from dead works to serve the living God?

Supporting Text: Hebrews 8:12

For I will be merciful to their unrighteousness, and their sins and their iniquities will I remember no more.

Comments & Questions:

- The blood of Jesus can purge your conscience.

- Under the New Testament, God has chosen to forget your sin.

- Do thoughts of past failures trouble you?

- Who is the accuser of the brethren?

Summary: As we partake of the bread and the blood we receive a revelation of the redemptive power of Christ that is more brilliant than any dark thought we may have had. The blood of Jesus covers our past and our outlook is bright.

MISSING THE MARK

Forgive Me for I Have Sinned

Supporting Text: Isaiah 53:10-11 [Study both verses]

> Yet it pleased the Lord to bruise him; he hath put him to grief: when *thou shalt make his soul an offering for sin,* he shall see his seed, he shall prolong his days, and the pleasure of the Lord shall prosper in his hand....

Supporting Text: 1 John 2:1-2

My little children, these things write I unto you, that ye sin not. And if any man sin, we have an advocate with the Father, Jesus Christ

the righteous: And he is *the propitiation for our sins:* and not for ours only, but also for the sins of the whole world.

Comments & Questions:

- Jesus is our sin offering, or atoning sacrifice.

- He is also our advocate who pleads on our behalf.

- Can you ever be good enough to make up for sin?

- If we do sin, what should we do about it?

Summary: This bread and wine represents Jesus, our sin offering. We are reminded that He died for us when we were yet lost in sin. Now, as the sons of God, He loves us no less. As we partake of His sacrifice we celebrate Him as our intercessor and advocate.

PARTNERSHIP

Joint Heirs With Jesus

Supporting Text: 1 Corinthians 1:9-10

God is faithful, by whom *ye were called unto the fellowship of his Son Jesus Christ our Lord.* Now I beseech you, brethren, by the name of our Lord Jesus Christ, that ye all speak the same thing, and that there be no divisions among you; but that ye be perfectly joined together in the same mind and in the same judgment.

Supporting Text: Philippians 2:3-9 [Study all seven verses]

...Look not every man on his own things, **but every man also on the things of others....**

Comments & Questions:

- We were called unto fellowship. Fellowship means partnership.

58

- We are in partnership with Jesus and with one another.

- How is Jesus working for our success?

- How can we work for the success of our partners?

Summary: At this table we are celebrating our partnership with one another through the body and blood of Jesus. Just as each member of a natural body works for the benefit of the other members, so we work for the benefit of our brethren. We solemnly pledge to help one another.

PERSECUTION

Ain't No Step for a High-Stepper

Supporting Text: John 15:18-20 [Study all three verses]

...If ye were of the world, the world would love his own: but because ye are not of the world, but *I have chosen you out of the world,* therefore the world hateth you....

Supporting Text: John 16:33

These things I have spoken unto you, that in me ye might have peace. In the world ye shall have tribulation: but be of good cheer; *I have overcome the world.*

Comments & Questions:

- Jesus was falsely accused and persecuted unto death.

- We cannot expect people in the world's system to love us.

- Jesus has overcome the world, and He has removed us from the world's system.

- Where is our place of safety and acceptance?

Summary: Jesus was forced to drink vinegar that we might drink from the cup of joy. His body was beaten and His hands and feet were pierced that we might be whole. As we receive this cup and this bread we are reminded He suffered persecution to redeem us to Himself. We are in a place of safety and acceptance; we are in the body of Christ.

PROTECTION

No Plague Will Come Nigh Your Dwelling

Supporting Text: Exodus 12:13

And the blood shall be to you for a token upon the houses where ye are: and when I see the blood, I will pass over you, and *the plague shall not be upon you to destroy you,* when I smite the land of Egypt.

Comments & Questions:

- The blood of the Passover Lamb over the door was a sign for the destroyer to pass over.

- The blood of Jesus establishes a line the enemy is forbidden to cross.

- How might a person step outside of the bloodline?

- How can we be sure we are safely under the blood?

Summary: Jesus is our Passover Lamb. His blood is over the doorpost of our hearts. As we share our Passover dinner we bring attention to the fact that God dwells within us. The blood of the Lamb covers us, and we can say, *Sickness, pass over this house; Death, pass over this house; Poverty, pass over this house.*

REUNION

I Will Never Leave Thee nor Forsake Thee

Supporting Text: 1 Corinthians 11:26

For as often as ye eat this bread, and drink this cup, ye do shew the Lord's death *till he come.*

Supporting Text: 2 Corinthians 5:6-9

Therefore we are always confident, knowing that, whilst we are at home in the body, we are absent from the Lord: (For we walk by faith, not by sight:) We are confident, I say, and willing rather to be absent from the body, and *to be present with the Lord.* Wherefore we labour, that, whether present or absent, we may be accepted of him.

Comments & Questions:

- Have you ever dealt with the fear of being left behind?

- Jesus longs to be with us just as we long to be with Him.

- We do not fear leaving this body because we know we will be present with Christ, and His saints, forever.

Summary: As we look upon these emblems we are reminded that Jesus promised, "...I will come again, and receive you unto myself..." (John 14:3). As we celebrate this feast we joyously anticipate feasting with Jesus in heaven at the marriage feast of the Lamb. Maranatha. Even so come quickly, Lord Jesus.

REVELATION

Sirs, We Would See Jesus!

Supporting Text: Luke 24:30-31

And it came to pass, as he sat at meat with them, he took bread, and blessed it, and brake, and gave to them. And *their eyes were opened,* and they knew him; and he vanished out of their sight.

Supporting Text: Ephesians 1:16-23 [Study all eight verses]

...That the God of our Lord Jesus Christ, the Father of glory, may give unto you *the spirit of wisdom and revelation* in the knowledge of him....

Comments & Questions:

- There are natural eyes and there are spiritual eyes.

- The Holy Spirit is the Spirit of revelation.

- What is your highest personal revelation of Jesus?

- What invisible things are around us now?

65

Summary: As we break this bread and drink from this cup, we pray that our eyes be opened that we may know more of Him. The Son of God is revealing Himself to us increasingly each day as we fellowship with Him in the Spirit.

SADNESS

Eat Thy Bread and Drink Thy Wine With Joy

Supporting Text: Hebrews 1:8-9

But unto the Son he saith, Thy throne, O God, is for ever and ever: a scepter of righteousness is the scepter of thy kingdom. Thou hast loved righteousness, and hated iniquity; therefore God, even thy God, hath anointed thee with *the oil of gladness* above thy fellows.

Supporting Text: Psalm 16:11

Thou wilt shew me the path of life: *in thy presence is fulness of joy;* **at thy right hand there are pleasures for evermore.**

Comments & Questions:

- Jesus was anointed with the oil of joy.

- Happiness, not sadness, best characterizes Jesus.

- How will you know you are on the path of life?

- How will you know when you are in God's presence?

Summary: This bread is the bread of life. The life and nature of Christ is in us. This cup is the cup of joy. Just as Jesus was anointed with the oil of gladness, so are we joyful. Because we know Him, we can, "Rejoice with joy unspeakable and full of glory" (1 Peter 1:8).

Separation

Ain't No Grave Gonna Hold This Body Down!

Supporting Text: John 16:16-22 [Study all seven verses]

> ...And ye now therefore have sorrow: but I will see you again, and your heart shall rejoice, and your joy no man taketh from you.

Supporting Text: John 6:53-56 [Study all four verses]

> ...Whoso eateth my flesh, and drinketh my blood, hath eternal life; and I will raise him up at the last day....

Comments & Questions:

- Jesus left His disciples briefly, but He returned to them after His resurrection.

- All who go to sleep in Jesus will rise again.

- Do you believe heaven is real?

- Who are you expecting to see in heaven?

Summary: As we partake of the flesh and blood of Jesus we are reminded that He was raised from the grave. As we eat, we remember His death, burial, and resurrection. We are celebrating the resurrection of the entire body of Christ, including those who have gone before us and we who follow.

SERVANT'S HEART

The Way Down Is the Way Up

Supporting Text: John 13:4-16 [Study all thirteen verses]

> ...If I then, your Lord and Master, have
> washed your feet; ye also ought to *wash one
> another's feet*....

Supporting Text: Philippians 2:5-8 [Study all four verses]

> But [Jesus] made himself of no reputation, and *took upon him the form of a servant,* and was made in the likeness of men.

Comments & Questions:

- Jesus is the Servant King.

- We are instructed to serve one another.

- Did serving people make Jesus any less noble or powerful?

- How many ways can we serve one another?

Summary: On the night He was betrayed, during the Last Supper, Jesus washed His disciples' feet. As we partake of the Lord's Table we are reminded that Jesus humbled Himself and became a servant. We recognize that His life and nature is in us by virtue of His body and blood.

TITHES

The Windows of Heaven Are Open!

Supporting Text: Genesis 14:18-20

And Melchizedek king of Salem brought forth *bread and wine:* and he was the priest of the most high God. And he blessed him, and said, Blessed be Abram of the most high God, possessor of heaven and earth: And blessed be the most high God, which hath delivered thine enemies into thy hand. And *he gave him tithes of all.*

Comments & Questions:

- The tithe is God's portion and it is holy.

- The tithing principle existed before the law, during the law, and after the law. It is a blessing, not a curse.

- Abram presented unto God a tenth of his increase as He partook of the priest's bread and the wine.

- Can we truly be partners with God if we deny Him His portion?

Summary: As we partake of the bread and the wine we remember that Jesus became poor so that we might become rich. Today we recognize, as our partner, He is entitled to His portion. This is holy communion. We share everything we have with Him because He has shared all He has with us.

UNITY

We Are One in the Spirit

Supporting Text: John 17:20-24 [Study all five verses]

...That *they all may be one; as thou, Father, art in me, and I in thee, that they also may be one in us: that the world may believe that thou hast sent me....*

Supporting Text: 1 Corinthians 12:23-27 [Study all five verses]

...And *whether one member suffer, all the members suffer with it; or one member be honoured, all the members rejoice with it....*

Comments & Questions:

- We are one because we are in the body of Christ.

- Just like in a natural body, each individual member affects the whole body of Christ.

- How would losing a hand, eye, or foot affect your body?

- How do you need those whom Christ has connected to you?

Summary: As we receive our portion of Christ's flesh and blood, we recognize that we are vitally connected to one another. We are reminded that Christ died for each of us and we live in Him. We are one because we are in fellowship with Him, and He is in each one of us.

Communion is a sacred Christian rite. The Lord personally gave it to us as a point of fellowship until He returns.

Family communion invites the very presence of the Lord into your household, sanctifying your surroundings, and flooding your environment with His peace. I pray that you will make family communion an ongoing part of your family life.

Larry Huggins
Ambassador

Endnotes

Chapter 2

[1] The words "community" and "communion" are derived from the Latin word for "common," *communis*. *Webster's New World™ College Dictionary*, 3d ed., s.v. "community," "communion," "common."

[2] *anaxios*: "irreverently." James E. Strong, "Greek Dictionary of the New Testament," in *Strong's Exhaustive Concordance of the Bible*: Biblesoft's New Exhaustive Strong's Numbers and Concordance with Expanded Greek-Hebrew Dictionary electronic database (copyright © 1994 by Biblesoft and International Bible Translators, Inc.) entry #371, 1 Corinthians 11:27.

[3] *krima*: "condemnation." Biblesoft's Strong's Greek-Hebrew Dictionary, entry #2917, 1 Corinthians 11:29.

[4] *diakrino*: "discern," "judge." Biblesoft's Strong's, entry #1252, 1 Corinthians 11:29.

[5] *diakrino*: "discern," "judge." Biblesoft's Strong's, entry #1252, 1 Corinthians 11:31.

6 *krino:* "condemn, damn," "judge": condemned,
   damned, judged. Biblesoft's Strong's, entry #2919, 1
   Corinthians 11:31.

7 *paideuo:* "educate," "discipline": educated, disciplined.
   Biblesoft's Strong's, entry #3811, 1 Corinthians 11:32.

8 *katakrino:* "condemn, damn": condemned, damned.
   Biblesoft's Strong's, entry #2632, 1 Corinthians 11:32.

About the Author

Rev. Larry Huggins is an ambassador to Mexico, the U.S.A., and the world. He has traveled to thousands of cities in more than fifty-six nations, planting gospel works and holding miracle crusades and seminars.

He and his wife, Loretta, reside in Central Mexico. They have four adult sons and, at this writing, one grandson. Together they operate Larry Huggins World Embassy, Incorporated (AKA Ambassador International Ministries, Inc.).

To contact Larry Huggins please write or call:

Ambassador Larry Huggins
Ambassador International Ministries, Inc.
3930 Glade Road, #108-387
Colleyville, TX 76034 USA
1-888-YES-LIFE
Or email him at:
larryhuggins@att.net

*Please include your prayer requests
and comments when you write.*

Prayer of Salvation

A born-again, committed relationship with God is the key to the victorious life. Jesus laid down His life and rose again so that we could spend eternity with Him in heaven and experience His absolute best on earth. If you would like to receive Jesus into your life in order to become born again, pray this prayer from your heart:

Heavenly Father, I come to You admitting that I am a sinner. Right now, I choose to turn away from sin, and I ask You to cleanse me of all unrighteousness. I believe that Your Son, Jesus, died on the cross to take away my sins. I also believe that He rose again from the dead so that I might be justified and made righteous through faith in Him. I call upon the name of Jesus Christ to be the Savior and Lord of my life. Jesus, I choose to follow You, and ask that You fill me with the power of the Holy Spirit. I declare that right now I am a child of God. I am free from sin, and full of the righteousness of God. I am saved in Jesus' name, Amen.

If you have prayed this prayer to receive Jesus Christ as your Savior, or if this book has changed your life, we would like to hear from you. Please write us at:

Harrison House Publishers
P.O. Box 35035
Tulsa, Oklahoma 74153

You can also visit us on the web at
www.harrisonhouse.com

Additional copies of this book
are available from your local bookstore.

HARRISON HOUSE
Tulsa, Oklahoma 74153